Australian Animals

Kangaroos

By Sara Louise Kras

Consulting Editor: Gail Saunders-Smith, PhD

Content Consultant: Bob Cleaver, owner
Wombat Rise Sanctuary, a home for rescued Australian wildlife
Sandleton, South Australia

Capstone
press

Mankato, Minnesota

Pebble Plus is published by Capstone Press,
151 Good Counsel Drive, P.O. Box 669, Mankato, Minnesota 56002.
www.capstonepress.com

 Books published by Capstone Press are manufactured with paper
containing at least 10 percent post-consumer waste.

Library of Congress Cataloging-in-Publication Data
Kras, Sara Louise.
    Kangaroos / by Sara Louise Kras.
    p. cm. — (Pebble plus. Australian animals)
    Includes bibliographical references and index.
    Summary: "Simple text and photographs present kangaroos, how they look, where they live,
and what they do" — Provided by publisher.
    ISBN-13: 978-1-4296-3311-6 (library binding)
    ISBN-13: 978-1-4296-3866-1 (pbk.)
1. Kangaroos — Juvenile literature. I. Title. II. Series.
QL737.M35K73 2010
599.2'22 — dc22   2008052557

Editorial Credits
Jenny Marks, editor; Bobbie Nuytten and Ted Williams, designers; Svetlana Zhurkin, media researcher

Photo Credits
DigitalVision, 1, 19
Getty Images/Photonica/Theo Allofs, 21
iStockphoto/VMJones, cover
Peter Arnold/Biosphoto/Régis Cavignaux, 17; John Cancalosi, 9
Shutterstock/BlueSoul Photography, 5, 13; Ralph Loesche, 7; Sharon Day, 15; Tijmen, 11

Note to Parents and Teachers

The Australian Animals set supports national science standards related to life science. This
book describes and illustrates kangaroos. The images support early readers in understanding
the text. The repetition of words and phrases helps early readers learn new words. This book
also introduces early readers to subject-specific vocabulary words, which are defined in the
Glossary section. Early readers may need assistance to read some words and to use the Table of
Contents, Glossary, Read More, Internet Sites, and Index sections of the book.

Table of Contents

Living in Australia

Australia has a mammal that hops up to 30 miles (48 kilometers) an hour. It's a furry kangaroo using its big back feet.

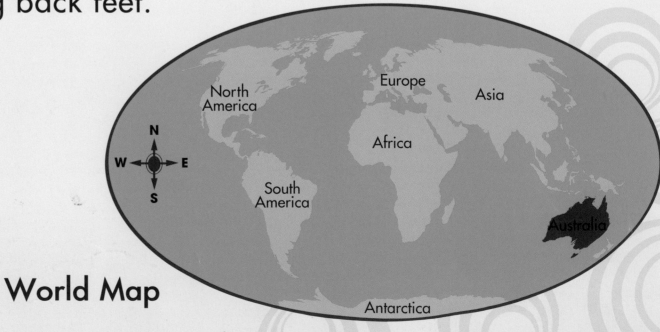

World Map

Some kangaroos live
in Australia's hot bush lands.
The rest live in forests
and grasslands.

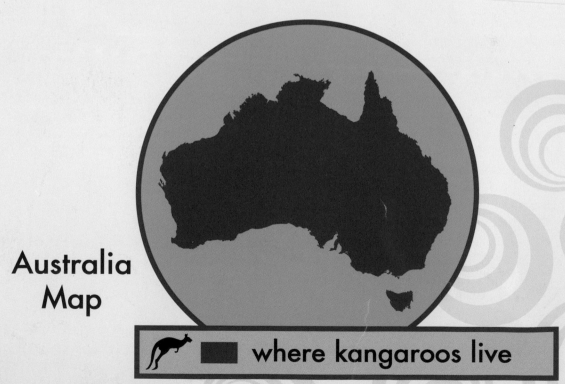

Australia
Map

where kangaroos live

Legs, Feet, and Tails

A kangaroo's long back legs
are made for jumping.
Kangaroos can travel
far and fast.

Kangaroos' front paws
have sharp claws.
They use their claws
to dig in the dirt.

Kangaroos have
big, thick tails.
They lean back
on their tails to balance.

Eating and Drinking

Kangaroos eat grass.

They can go a long time without water.

Eating grass gives kangaroos some of the water they need.

Growing up

Kangaroos are marsupials.
Female kangaroos have
pouches on their bellies.
Their newborn babies
grow in the pouches.

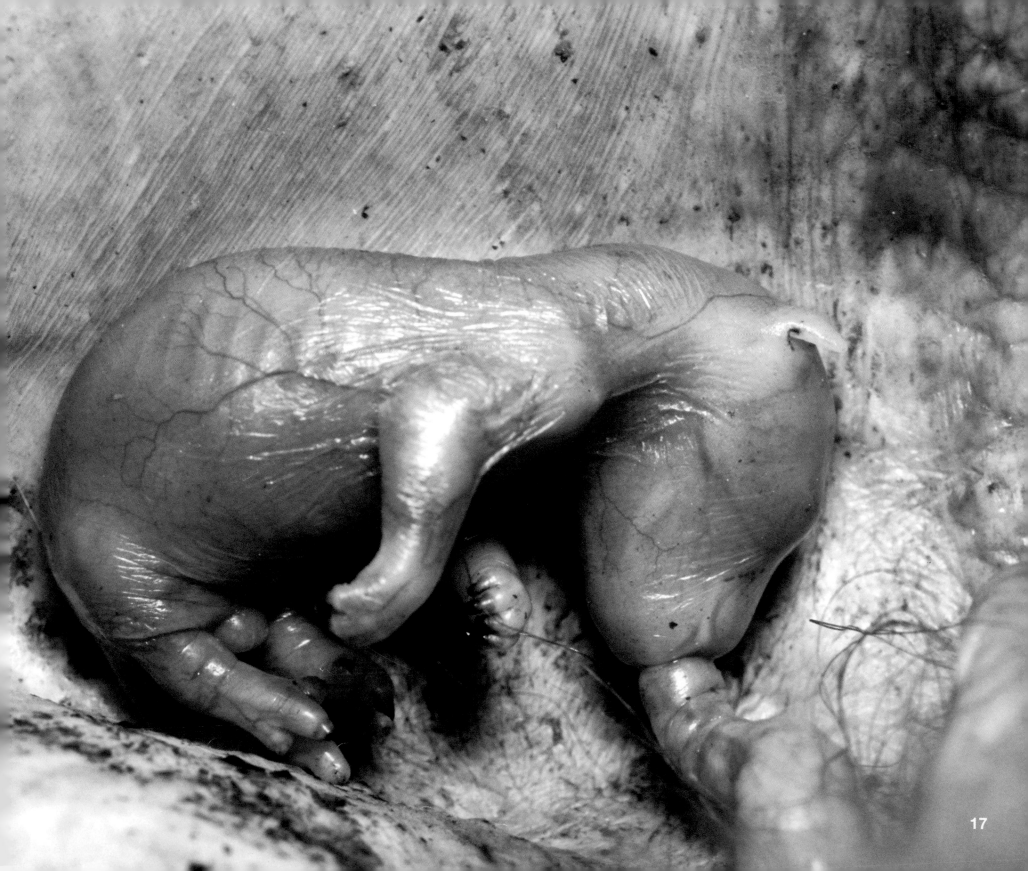

Young kangaroos
are called joeys.

For up to 10 months, joeys stay
in their mothers' pouches.

Kangaroos live up to 20 years.

Staying Safe

Some kangaroos form mobs.

One male kangaroo
is the leader of the group.

He watches for predators
and keeps the mob safe.

Glossary

balance — to keep steady and not fall over

bush lands — a somewhat dry part of Australia where trees and shrubs grow

joey — a young kangaroo

mammal — a warm-blooded animal that has a backbone and hair or fur; female mammals feed milk to their young.

marsupial — a kind of animal that carries its young in a pouch on its stomach

mob — a group of kangaroos that live together; each mob has up to 20 kangaroos.

pouch — a pocket-like flap of skin

predator — an animal that hunts other animals for food

Read More

Arnold, Caroline. *A Kangaroo's World.* Caroline Arnold's Books. Minneapolis: Picture Window Books, 2008.

Sill, Cathryn P. *About Marsupials: A Guide for Children.* Atlanta: Peachtree, 2006.

Spilsbury, Louise and Richard. *Watching Kangaroos in Australia.* Wild World. Chicago: Heinemann, 2006.

Internet Sites

FactHound offers a safe, fun way to find Internet sites related to this book. All of the sites on FactHound have been researched by our staff.

Here's all you do:

Visit *www.facthound.com*

FactHound will fetch the best sites for you!

Index

Word Count: 163
Grade: 1
Early-Intervention Level: 24

Search dogs use their eyes, ears, and nose to search. They can find someone buried under 13 feet (4 meters) of snow.

Training

Search dogs train

for one to three years.

They learn to climb ladders.

They walk across beams.

Search dogs practice looking for people. When they sniff out the person, they get a toy. The dogs think it's a game, like hide-and-seek.

On the Job

Search dogs are daring workers.

They walk over piles of debris.

They search in the dark

and in bad weather.

Many search dogs work
for six to seven years.
These amazing dogs work
hard to save lives.